Pebble® **Plus**

Mighty Machines

Semitrucks

by Matt Doeden

Consulting Editor: Gail Saunders-Smith, PhD

Consultant: Sandy Hurlbut, President
Transportation Center for Excellence
Eagan, Minnesota

Capstone *press*®

Mankato, Minnesota

Pebble Plus is published by Capstone Press,
151 Good Counsel Drive, P.O. Box 669, Mankato, Minnesota 56002.
www.capstonepub.com

Books published by Capstone Press are manufactured with paper
containing at least 10 percent post-consumer waste.

Library of Congress Cataloging-in-Publication Data
Doeden, Matt.
    Semitrucks / by Matt Doeden.
    p. cm.—(Pebble plus. Mighty machines)
    Summary: "Simple text and photographs present semitrucks, their parts, and how drivers use
them"—Provided by publisher.
    Includes bibliographical references and index.
    ISBN-13: 978-0-7368-6356-8 (hardcover)
    ISBN-10: 0-7368-6356-7 (hardcover)
1. Tractor trailer combinations—Juvenile literature. I. Title: Semi trucks. II. Title. III. Series: Pebble plus. Mighty
machines.
TL230.15.D645 2007
629.224—dc22   2006000514

Editorial Credits
Amber Bannerman, editor; Molly Nei, set designer; Patrick D. Dentinger, book designer;
    Jo Miller, photo researcher; Scott Thoms, photo editor

Photo Credits
Capstone Press/TJ Thoraldson Digital Photography, cover (truck), 4–5, 6–7, 10–11, 12–13
Corbis/zefa/Roland Gerth, 20–21
The Image Finders/Mark E. Gibson, 16–17
Photodisc, cover (fruit)
Shutterstock/David Gaylor, 1
UNICORN Stock Photos/Jeff Greenberg, 9; Martin R. Jones, 18–19; Ted Rose, 14–15

**Capstone Press would like to thank Rob Alvarado (page 10) and the Westman Freightliner company in
    Mankato, Minnesota, for their assistance with photo shoots for this book.**

Note to Parents and Teachers

The Mighty Machines set supports national standards related to science, technology, and
society. This book describes and illustrates semitrucks. The images support early readers in
understanding the text. The repetition of words and phrases helps early readers learn new
words. This book also introduces early readers to subject-specific vocabulary words, which
are defined in the Glossary section. Early readers may need assistance to read some words
and to use the Table of Contents, Glossary, Read More, Internet Sites, and Index sections of
the book.

Printed in the United States of America in North Mankato, Minnesota.
042011   006128R

Table of Contents

What Are Semitrucks?

Semitrucks are
big, strong trucks.
They pull trailers
and deliver goods to stores.

Semitruck Parts

The front part
of a semitruck
is called the tractor.

The engine is in the tractor.

engine

The trailer hooks onto

the back of the tractor.

The trailer holds boxes

of food, clothing,

and other goods.

9

Most semitrucks

have 18 wheels.

Some have 10 wheels.

The driver sits in the cab.
All the truck's controls
are inside the cab.

What Semitrucks Do

Semitrucks pull heavy loads.

They move cars

from place to place.

Some semitrucks
haul tankers.
Tankers are filled with
gasoline or other liquids.

Some semitrucks

carry buildings.

They may even

haul other trucks.

Mighty Semitrucks

A semitruck
pulls a heavy load.
Semitrucks are
mighty machines.

Glossary

cab—an enclosed area of a truck or other vehicle where the driver sits

engine—a machine that makes the power needed to move something

goods—the items people buy, sell, and use; semitrucks deliver goods to stores.

haul—to pull or carry a load

tanker—a trailer that holds liquids, such as gasoline or milk

trailer—the part of a semitruck where goods are loaded and carried

Read More

Armentrout, David, and Patricia Armentrout. *Trucks.* Transportation. Vero Beach, Fla.: Rourke, 2004.

Ransom, Candice F. *Big Rigs.* Pull Ahead Books. Minneapolis: Lerner, 2005.

Werther, Scott P. *Big Rigs.* Reading Power. New York: PowerKids Press, 2002.

Internet Sites

FactHound offers a safe, fun way to find Internet sites related to this book. All of the sites on FactHound have been researched by our staff.

Here's how:

1. Visit *www.facthound.com*

2. Choose your grade level.

3. Type in this book ID **0736863567** for age-appropriate sites. You may also browse subjects by clicking on letters, or by clicking on pictures and words.

4. Click on the **Fetch It** button.

FactHound will fetch the best sites for you!

Index

Word Count: 114
Grade: 1
Early-Intervention Level: 14